Your Kiss

Your kiss has captured my soul
So full of passion and intense
Your lips so soft and inviting
Your tongue sweet and satisfying
The melding of your lips to mine is electrifying
I feel it in every muscle
My temperature rises making me hot
My heart hastens making me oh so eager
I am lost in you for that moment in time
When you and I are one
Joined in passion
Joined in desire
Joined in anticipation of what's to come
Your kiss is a precursor to ecstasy
A Pavlovian trigger to my body and mind
I pine for it
I require it
I require you

Focus on Me

Starting over again
Learning again
Hurting again
Wanting again
Maybe just maybe
Loving again
Alone
Not an option
Desires
Needs
Companionship
Attention
Affection
Requirements
What now
Which way do I go
Where do I turn
Who will I find
Why bother
Needs that require fulfilling
I want so much
But nothing
I'm lost at home
Confused
I'm waiting for something
But not sure what
I looking for something
But don't know where to search
I want to be alone
I want clear thoughts
I need to think

Focus on what I need
Focus on what I want
Focus on me

I'm Sorry

I apologize for being who I am
Please forgive what I have become
I yearn to be free and untethered
You have your faults
And I mine
I persevered and claimed you as my own
I was relentless, possessed
I gave you no choice but to love me
You were all there was for me
All I wanted
You were
Were
I tried to maintain keep what was from slipping away
I tried to stop the feelings from changing
I tried to keep the desire
I tried
Now
What was is gone
Now only indifference remains
You are a man wanted by most
Desired by many
I appreciate you and love you
But my heart is no longer in it
The spell is broken and I see
We have drifted and aligned away from center
You cannot see me
I wonder if you ever did
With you I have grown
I have learned what could possibly be
I am better because of you
Now, I must go and become me as I should and want to be

You Say You Love Me

You say you love me
How
You don't know me
You know the feel of my touch
The taste of my kiss
The heat of my passion
But you don't know me
You don't know the way I think
The way I behave when sick
The way I act when angry
You speculate what you think I may be
You envision what you want me to be
What I am I have shown you
I hide nothing
I do not pretend or put on airs
I eat when hungry
I sleep when tired
I can devour when aroused
I love with reckless abandon
I am insatiable when excited
When I am done
When I have had enough
When you no longer satiate me
I turn
No longer will I give all of me
No longer will I succumb to your will
No longer will the desire dictate
I may not leave but I am gone
My blueprint is simple
My love available and carefree
What I am I have shown you
You ask what you want of me
I give what I can

Don't take more than what is offered
Don't see more than there is
You say you love me
Now show me you can

What Now

What now
The words have been said
The feelings validated and reciprocated
You belong to one
I to another
Stolen moments no longer suffice
Time shared is precious but never enough
The longing grows with each day
Thoughts are hazy and rampant
Soon the pain will start
The anger will grow and engulf
Jealousy
Grief
Sadness
Eventually loss will ensue
What then
Will it survive the journey
Will we want to
Only time will tell

Uh Oh

Uh oh
It has started
The downward spiral
The spiral that leads to expulsion
The expulsion of you from my heart
I warned you
Warned that a crack was developing
I begged you to heed
Heed the crevice that was forming
You should never have censored me
Allowed me to get an arms length away
Allowed me to ponder what really is
The glasses are off and the mind has taken over
I see the flaws
The selfishness
The lack of consideration
The control
I now see what truly is
I guess what always was
I realize that I'm not the one for you
I would have left what I helped build
For you
I felt what words could not describe
With you
I wanted to be always
In you
I saw a future
Now the dust has cleared
You said your peace
I was wrong
Wrong to think
You were the one
Wrong to feel
We could ever be more
I thought you understood

I felt we were connected
I was wrong
Now I know
You are not my one
You are what you are
A man
Like any other
A face in the crowd
An encounter that will leave no imprint

Tomorrow

Tomorrow I see a brighter day
Yesterday is gone never to return
Today is too close to see and understand
Tomorrow is what I look towards
For then I will see what yesterday had become
What did I do and accomplish
What do I need to do and achieve
Yesterday is gone never to return
Today is here and too close to see
Tomorrow is what I look forward to and strive towards
Because tomorrow is where I will be once today is gone

Yesterday

    I'm thinking of a time not long ago
        A time of struggle and strife
        A time of chaos and unrest
     A time of desperation and need
    A time of discord and animosity
          I was thinking about
             YESTERDAY

How I Know

I know what I know
Because I've seen what I've seen
I do as I do
Because I've been where I've been
I am who I am
Because I've done as I've done
I act as I act
Because I know I can
I am me as I will always be
No more no less
Me, as I am meant to be

Who Knew

Who knew
It started with a kiss
A gentle mesh of your lips to mine
A commingling of sweet nectar And sharing of a breath
Who knew
How much I would long for the taste of you
Crave the feel of your touch
Who knew
It would start an ember burning deep inside
Igniting a fire that would blaze so blue
Who knew
The mere thought of you would make butterflies twitter
Who knew
I would love you

Drained

The night we shared was draining
I'm drained of debilitating thoughts
I'm drained of emptiness
I'm drained of pain
I'm drained of longing
Drained of everything
Now with you
I want to be fulfilled
Filled with anticipation
Overflowing with passion
Spilling over with desire
I want to drown in your essence
I want you and all you have to offer

Fickle

I wish I knew what I should do
I desire companionship
Yet like being alone
I desire commitment and stability
But run feeling suffocated and caged
I need love
Yet I act hard and bitter
I long to be loved and desired
But reject advances
I starve for affection and attention
Yet turn a deaf ear to compliments and accolades
So filled with self-pity and disdain
I fear solitude

All of You

Alone I sit remembering you
I can still feel your touch on my body
My chest heavy from the weight of you
My lips still tender from your passionate kiss
My senses still reeling from your scent
I feel you with me
Yet you are not
I again long for your embrace
I enjoy being with you
Your presence excites me
The thought of you consoles me
The more I'm with you the more I want to be with you
I know how you are
But, I still want you
I still need you
I need what you have to give
I want all of you
Your touch electrifies me
Your kiss melts my heart
Your words touch my soul
Your gaze can see the real me
I think of you and warmth engulfs
I see you and my eyes smile
When you wrap your arms around me my will weakens
I want to give you all of me

The Last Time

The last time I saw you
My eyes welled with tears
The last time I kissed you
My lips quivered with pleasure
The last time I held you near
My heart skipped a beat
The last time I loved you
My body exploded in ecstasy
The last time I thought of you
My mind reeled with possibilities and expectations
The last time we talked
My heart broke
Because the last time
Was the last time
There is too much left to be said
There is so much we needed to do
There were so many experiences left unshared
The last time
Wasn't supposed to be the last time
The next time
Was supposed to be the beginning

We Prevailed

A year has passed
Though filled with much turmoil and strife
We prevailed
Though battered, beaten, and slightly worn
We prevailed
Love is the key
Hope the answer
Armed with these defenses
We will always prevail
Because all that I am
All that I will ever be
Is nothing
Without you in my life
This I vow to you
Your wife for life

Love Is

Love is not limited to the bound body
It transcends the body and earthly plane
Nothing can change what you feel inside
No physical being or act can change its true embodiment
It must take its course
Deeper than comprehension
Stronger than earthly ties
Beyond explanation
Love is Faith

Where Do You Go

When the body fails
When the mind shuts down
Where do they go
When the spirit dies
When the thoughts and memories slip away
Where do they go
What becomes of the broken spirit
What mends a truly broken heart
Where do you go when your lost and adrift
When peace is out of reach
Where can you go
There is no running from the despair
No where to hide from what must be
Escape is impossible
So when the body fails
When the mind shuts down
You just Go On

Happy Birthday

Today is your birthday
The day of your birth
The day you opened your eyes to this earth
You smiled your first smile
And cried your first cry
What a great day
For years you've walked this place
Made your mark
Left your grace
Today is your birthday
Smile your smile
Cry if you like
Just know it is the next day towards the rest of
your life
Happy Birthday

What If We Had No History

What if we had no history
Where would the prejudice come from
What would we draw our hates and fears from
Would we have to see the world through different
unclouded eyes
What if we had no history
Wouldn't we have to judge others on their merits
and personalities
What if skin was clear and all that was visible was
the inside
Would the prejudice, bias and hate still exist
It is understood that what is unknown is feared
So how can a simple color, race, religion, creed, or
sex be so misunderstood
What if we started today
Would the differences be so apparent
I'm not so sure they would
Without that wealth of bigotry and hate to draw
upon the differences would not be so clear
What if we had no history
I feel that we would be better and able to see
Anyway, That's just me

Too Late

I hate this
I hurt you
I touched your soul and scarred it
Your heart belonged to me
I broke it
I honestly didn't know
I never wanted this
I always wanted you
I thought I had it figured out
I know now I didn't
It seems I never knew
Unfortunately now it's too late to care

Heartfelt Apology

Don't be sorry
Just don't do it anymore
Don't apologize for what was meant
Don't feign sympathy where none exist
Be who you are
What you are
The rabid wolf in sheep's clothing
The flea ridden dog at his Master's feet
Infesting while pretending subordination
So I say
Don't be sorry
Be who you are
What you are
Apologize for nothing

Ambiguity

I thought about you today
I felt pain and elation
I thought we could make it work
Then I thought we could never truly be
I felt sadness and hope
I thought all my dreams had been answered
Then I thought this can never last
I felt the warm comforting embrace of your love
And then the crushing asphyxiation of mine
I thought you were everything I wanted
Then I thought I can't do this
I wanted you to be all I needed
I knew you were all I desired
Then I knew I hated being without you
I felt with you I couldn't be happier
Then I felt the numbing pain of your absence
I believe I am truly in love with you
And I believe you can truly devastate me
I felt a glimmer of hope
And the weight of reality
You can make me feel at ease and optimistic
Then you can leave me feeling distraught and empty

Won't Give Up

I'm tired.
I think
I need to walk away
I'm sure
I have to let go
I've resolved
I should stop loving you
I will
I must forget about you
I've decided
I'm going to move on
I am
But
My legs won't move
I'm trying
My mind won't rest
Even in sleep
My heart won't give up
My mind is pushing me to retreat
My body is pulling for me to concede
I want so much to move on
But I can't
I have to play through
I have to remove every vestige of hope
I must see it to the end
I know we're close
I know the end is imminent
But
As long as a scintilla of you runs through me
I must keep trying
I can't let go

Theft

I know
I know what I've done
I know what I'm doing
I never meant to harm her
I never wanted him to know
I can't change what has been done
I can't stop now
It has all gone too far
I won't be without him
The thought of it
Well, I just don't think of it
He is mine now

How Could You

How could you
How could you kill
What lies deep inside
How could you destroy
What can't be touched
How could you steal
What was once safe and secure
How could you crush
What seemed indestructible
How could you
Why did you
Destroy what was so good and true
It was to me
I guess not to you
How could you
Why would you

How Do You Say It

How do you say I love you
When words fail to work
My heart aches for your love
My body yearns for your touch
My hands reach for the emptiness where you once stood
How do I express my feelings
When I can't speak
The words elude me
And the thoughts and feelings choke me
How do I make you see
What my eyes see in you
My heart feels for you
My body wants from you
My mind gets from you
The words escape me
The feelings strangle me
The thoughts bind me
I can't make you see
You have to know
Because you know me

Betrayal

Betrayal
A wicked word
A worse act
Murder with no weapon
Destruction with no debris
Total annihilation of all that was
With a single act
With a single word
I am sorry
Does not repair the damage that has been done
I love you
Does not mean what it used to
Forgive
Yes
Truly
No
Forget
Impossible
Betrayal
Is a wicked word
And an even worse act

Expectations

Everyone has them
No one can reach them
Disappointment is imminent
Jubilation a joke
Lower them
You lower yourself
Raise them
You stand alone
It is a no win situation
Or is it
Depend on yourself
No one else
Depend on yourself
You know what to expect
Depend on yourself

Happy I Am

Happy I am
Happy I will be
I have finally found someone for me
He wants what I want
He needs what I need
Will it last
I hope so indeed
I have flaws
He has faults
Life is not as perfect as I may have thought
Sometimes we discuss
Sometimes we fuss
But in life that is a must
All in all
I am happy
I am gay
Hope this will last forever and a day

Share A Dream With Me

Share a dream with me
Be my guide in all this misery
Bring to light what I cannot see
Shield me from harm
Protect my spirit
Chase away my fears
Make possible my dreams
Walk a path with me
Enhance my feelings
Explore my thoughts
Share a world with me
Make it what we want it to be
Make a life with me
For with you is where I want and need to be
You are in my dreams
You are my life
You are my world
Share my dreams with me

Different

Why must different mean bad
To say something is different is to say
That is new
That is beautiful
That is inventive and gay
To say something is different is to say
I am in awe
I am impressed
I am enlightened and better to have known
To say something is different does not imply
You should be afraid
You should hide
You should hate and fight
To truly be different is a blessing
To truly be different is an awakening an awareness
of all that we are or ever shall become
To be different is to be alive and living
Different I am
Different I will always hope to be
IF I AM LUCKY

Passing of Time

Time is dragging
Taking with it every ounce of security
Slowly it moves
When needs are great
Quickly it goes
When time is of the essence
When will time and necessity compromise
When I need more time
I get less
When I need time to fly
It drags out and prolongs
I need some nights to last forever
They are gone with the speed of light
When if ever will we be in sync
So much needs to be done
Even more needs accomplished

Pledge

Today I pledge anew
What is only for you
My heart
My soul
The love inside that grows stronger with each passing day
To lose your love would be to lose myself
What I feel for you is beyond words
What you feel for me is beyond understanding
What I know is that what I feel is all that I am
All that I want to be
You are in my thoughts every night and day
I sit here and think of you
I feel your voice
As you sing to me
I sense your gaze
As it stares upon me
I experience your touch
Every time you caress my body
I am overwhelmed
I am enthralled
I am lost in you
As your essence surrounds and covers me
I am alone without you
I reach for you
But you are not within my grasp
I need you
Ache for you
Yearn for you
Husband you are my everything
My life

Can't Stand What You Do To Me

I can't stand what you do to me
You fill my life with misery
You bring me up
Then snatch me down
You make me feel safe and secure
Then throw me to the dogs
I hate what you do to me
You squeeze my heart
And erode my soul
I feel love
I feel confusion and disdain
You hold me tight
Then you steal my breath
Your killing me
Every minute of every day
Your hurting me
With every lie that you tell
Your destroying me
With every promise you break
Continue
There soon will be nothing left of me
My body, mind, heart, and soul
Can't take what you do to me
Please
Stop stealing my security
Because soon there will be nothing left of me

I Hate You

I hate you
For the way you make me feel
I hate your eyes
Your face
Your tears
You lie with your forked tongue
And promise with your hollow heart
Your soul and voice leave no trace
You cast no shadow
You speak only in whispers
Where you once stood only slime remains
I spit out your name
And shun your embrace

Alone Again

What I want
What I need
Not what I get
Not what I have
What to do
Where to go
I thought I knew
I don't know
I haven't a clue
Somber
Some
Misled
Maybe
Confused
Completely
Alone
Again

Games

Games are stupid
Games are a waste of time
They frustrate
They teach you nothing
And try your patience
Emotional games
Lack a playing forum
There are no rules
No rules mean
NOT fair
To play is
To lose
To initiate is
To seek a failure
To initiate is
To start a fools errand
Emotional Games
No one wins
Everyone ends up
Alone

If Only You Knew

If only you knew
What I know
You wouldn't do
What you do
You wouldn't think
What you think
You wouldn't assume
What you do not know
If only you saw
What I see
You would never question me
You would feel what I feel
Know what I know
See what I see
You would just love me for me
Not what you think me to be
If only you knew
What I know
You would feel like SHIT

Decisions

Choices made under duress
Should I
Could I
Do I even want to
Am I happy
Or just settling
Can I be happy
Should I even try
What to do
How to act
What to think
Don't know
Unsure
Too many decisions
Choices to be made under duress

For Pity's Sake

To be alone
What I must be
I have no one
And no one wants me
I have love to give
And no one to accept
I have a heart that aches
Arms that yearn
When will they ever learn
There is more to me
Much more than what they see

Alone

Alone I am
Alone I'll be
Not knowing who to love
Or who will love me
Choosing wrong
Without a thought
Choosing Right
Never
Naught
I don't know how to be anyway but alone
So, alone I am
Alone I will be

Friends

Friends
A treasure
A find
One lost to me
Can't make them
Can't find them
How
Why
Lack of patience
Lack of will
No, I just don't know how
To handle
To deal
Will I ever know
The treasure
The find

Wit's End

Can't take the stress
Can't handle the pain
Can't rebel
Can't protest
Must only deal
Handle whatever comes
Stop coming
Too much at once
Coming from all directions
Going but one place
They won't go away
I can only adjust
I'll settle
I'll deal
Without complaint
Only Silence

Do You Care

Can you tell what hurts me
Do you know what I am feeling
Can you say you love me
Do you even care

Why must you let me go on
Day after day
Night after night
Making a fool of myself
Is it for your amusement
Do you enjoy what you see
Do you know what you do
Do you even care

This is really stupid
Do you know how dumb
Or Maybe you already do
What is truly inside of me
What I could really do
But know this
I do care

I've done what I've done
I've said what I've said
Nothing can change the past
Nothing can make you truly aware
Nothing or no one could make you care

Obsessive, Compulsive

Obsessive
Compulsive
I'm not sure I know how to be happy
It's been so long
I find fault in all around me
Yet, there possibly is none
I find reason for sadness
Though none exists
I trust no one
But, love so easily
I feel deeply
Too deeply
So deeply as to cause pain
Unnecessary
Yet, unavoidable
Obsessive
Compulsive
I guess I am

Anticipation of Beginning

I want you so much
I can't sleep
I can't think straight
My mind wanders with thoughts of you
My arms ache to hold and embrace you
My lips quiver awaiting your touch
My body, well my body just yearns
I want these feelings to ebb, pass, or go away
Just so I can make it through the day
I miss the warmth I can't share
I miss the arms that used to hold me
Hell, I just miss you
I want to spend my nights in your arms
And days in your gaze
I need to escape this abyss of emptiness and loneliness
As long as I breathe I ache
Until I am back in your embrace
I want the different world to go away
So, We can begin our life

Wishing for Recognition

I wish I could understand
I wish I had a clue
I need something more
I have felt immense in your arms
I have been shrunken by your touch
I wish I knew what I was doing
Where I was going
I wish I could let it go
Not think
Not feel
Not be
But I am
I can't stop
Missing you
Loving you
Wanting you
Needing you
Hating you
It's true
I hate you
I hate the pain you caused
The tears that have fallen
The sleep that has been lost
I hate I love you so much
It hurts
Why don't you need me

I Wonder

Moments like these I wonder
I wonder how
How things came to be this way
I wonder why
Why do things seem to be going in this direction
I wonder when
When will it all come together and make sense
Moments like these I think
I think I know how
How I can make a change
I think I know why
Why things need to change
I think I know when
Now
Sometimes I sit in wonder and think
What am I going to do with my life
How am I going to do it
When am I going to do it
Now seems to be the right time
I just have to wait
For the how to be revealed
Until then I'll sit and wonder
I'll sit and think
And wait for moments like these to pass

Love 101

I want to be in love
But I don't know how
I want to feel unconditional love and understanding
But I can't let go
I want to know true bliss
But I can't open up
Am I doomed to live my life behind these walls
Not feeling the warmth of loving companionship
Fearing the gaze and touch of another
Alone
Misunderstood
Where is the light in this bleak existence
I want to give warmth
But only cold emanates
I want to understand
But only indifference shows
I want happiness
But only sullenness and despondency prevails
I don't want to be alone
But that is where I am
That is the only place I am heading

Jester's Song

What a fool I am
I guess I always will be
A fool for love
A fool for hope
A fool for possibilities
One day I'll learn
Love hurts
Hope stings
Possibilities deceive
Reality is the only truth
Open your eyes
Close your heart
Suppress your feelings
Learn
Learn from the past
Learn from the pain
Learn from the lessons
Live
Live in today
Live in reality

I Am Me

I am who I am
Because I am me
Born to be
What I have become
Destined to live
How I have lived
Fated to deal
With my predetermined fate
Birth made me
Fate molded me
Destiny determines me
Life challenges me
I am who I am
Because I am me

Merry Christmas

Christmas supposedly a wondrous time
A time for joyous celebration
A time to reveal in the wonder that is life
Why
This day is no different than any other
A day in any month
A month in any year
A year in any lifetime
A lifetime in any existence
Why
Does the sun shine any brighter
Do the moments last any longer
Do the feelings really change
Do problems simply fade away at the stroke of midnight
No
Nothing changes
It only gets buried under mounds of wrapping paper and ribbons
Choices still remain to be made
Paths still need to be chosen
Mistakes yet to be made
Christmas
Changes nothing
Only delays the inevitable
Life
Remember
It is just any day in any month in any year of any lifetime

Moment of Clarity

I had a thought once
A clear concise vision
An idea of what could and should be
It dissipated
As a storm cloud on a sunny day
I had a dream once
Both realistic and achievable
Seemed to be what should be
It dissolved
As a snowflake in a warm palm
Thoughts, dreams, ideas, visions
All seem so possible
But when brought into the light
They fade

Slow Boil

A heat wells inside me
A thirst awaiting quenching
I need relief
I need food for the hunger
Reins for this wild abandon
I need you
Your strong arms enveloping me
Your throbbing manhood inside of me
Your passionate kiss releasing me
The thought of you excites me
Your touch sends my body reeling
My mind is awash with images of you

Truth

Before the time will come
When darkness comes to light
You will see all fears
You will sense all anguish
You will feel all apprehension
Dispel
You will know in your heart
You will understand in your mind
You will sense in your soul
Truth

Caught Between Love and Lust

When you love one
Can you truly love another
My mind tells me
No
My heart and body tell me another
When said to me
It wasn't true
Now
I'm doing the same to you
Because love for one is always stronger
The one I desire and lust with my body will fade
The one I love with my heart and mind will last longer
The one I truly love
Is you

Time

Time they say
Heals all wounds
Only to have them reopen again and again
Time they say
Makes all things better
Don't they know time only slows when you are in pain
They say
Forgive and forget
However they don't realize the more you forget the more you have to forgive
Because with time only you change
Everyone else stays the same
They just change faces
So you see
Time changes nothing but the years
The pain never goes away
It just goes below
Until the next time

Something

Between now and never
Someplace near here and there
At a time before infinity
Something changed
Neither for better nor worse
Not really good or bad
Just different
Nothing specific or precise
A shift in air and space
A Slight shiver on the spine of complacency
Some presence where once there was none
Seems like something
Maybe it's nothing
Its just that something is different

Intriguing You Are

Words escape me
Why You
Why Me
You possess an energy
An air about you
A silent sexuality
My desire for you grows
My thoughts are stolen by you
My dreams encroached on
You have become the air I breathe
The rhythm to which I beat
You have saturated my senses
You intrigue me
Still
Words escape what you have become to me
Why here
Why now
Why You
Lucky I suppose

Decide Already

I need to think
I need to assess
I want to be alone
I want to choose
I want my life back
Content is not enough
Nothing wrong is not everything
I'm not sure what can be done
I'm not sure what I can do
I want to walk away
How do I walk away
Can I walk away
When do I walk away
Will I walk away

Love Hurdles

I would love to love you
But the obstacles are too many
The road too rough
You keep me at such a distance
True emotion and feeling are impossible
You show no fear
You show no love
You show that you do no care to care
You are heartless, cruel, and unfeeling
You smile with your false benevolence
You hug with arms devoid of sympathy
Your delicate touch burns with indifference
I am caught in your spell of confusion
Trapped in your pit of false dreams and ideas
The fault is mine
For you need to bear no burden
You said you wouldn't care
I didn't believe you could remain so cold
You said you weren't ready to love
I couldn't believe you would be so unyielding
You said Do what you have to do
I could not give up the fight
I still can't stop trying, hurting, feeling, or caring
You still remain unfazed
I must go
Go
Because distance is freedom

I Suppose I Knew

I felt it coming
I felt it slowly slipping away
The looks changed
The feel of the touch had lost something
Before I couldn't name it I just knew
I knew something was different
When we loved it no longer left me feeling warm
The coldness started creeping in
The space between us where once there wasn't one grew
I knew I felt it I couldn't name it
I just knew The laughs decreased
The tension grew
The talking has stopped
The tears have begun to flow
I knew
I would feel it
I didn't know you could see it
I never would have guessed you could touch it
The point when love starts slipping away
It is a physical tangible thing

Love's Genesis

The time we have spent has been passion filled and blissful
The fire I feel right now is strong and burns bright
I can not comprehend or extinguish
I feel alive and vibrant but
Words cannot truly describe the feelings you have evoked in me
My mind reels when I think of you
My body yearns from the mere whisper of your name
Your voice to me is melodious and arouses every nerve in my body
Your touch sends waves of tremors through me and I feel weak and vulnerable
So quickly time has passed and allowed this seed to grow and blossom
I feel as if it will last but a flash and be an after thought of times gone by
I wish this feeling could last and burn with the fire and force of a star in the sky
Reality is sobering and time has never been a friend
For now I'll bask in your flame so bright and white
I'll swim in the deepness of your words
I'll be swaddled in the strength of your touch
For Now
For now nothing else is as we are
For now no one else matters
For now you and I are
FOR NOW

What's Wrong

What's wrong
Why feel this way
The sky is still blue
The grass is still green
The sun is shining so brightly
So, why feel this way
Why feel so alone and empty
Why feel it's so dark and desolate
Why feel as if nothing matters
Why feel so wrong when everything is going so right
Why cry in the sunshine
Why frown when birds sing
Why dismiss all that is beautiful
Why feel this way
What's wrong

Tantrum

I wish I knew what to do
My mind toils
My heart aches
I'm scared lonely and forlorn
The man I think I want
Feels not the same for me
I want passion's fire
I want love's warmth
I want
I want
I want what I can never have

When

When will it all come together
When will time and place mesh
When will person and feelings collide
When will it all make sense
When the time is right
Your not
When you are ready
The time has past
When time is plentiful
Love is elusive
When love is overwhelmingly abundant
Time is scarce
When will it all come together
Reality says
It won't
Heart says
It must
Person, Time, and Place in unison
Harmony and happiness abound
Maybe Someday
Probably Never
Never in THIS LIFETIME BECAUSE THE HEART LIES
ALL THE STINKING TIME

Anger's Origin

When I am angry
It comes from deep inside
I feel it in my arms
I feel it in my toes
I feel it in my fingers
I even feel it in my nose
I tell you this for just one reason
You're the ROOT of this anger

What Do You Know

No one knows
No one understands
The hurt
The pain
The torture of ignorance
The torture of knowing
The inability to stop what is bad
The ability to let it continue
How do you stop the heart?
With the mind
No, it's lost
Distracted
Only solution
Time
However, it doesn't heal
Only buries
Pain of the heart NEVER heals, only scars

Relinquish and Accept

Again I have tried
Again I have failed
Caring for another
Who can care for no one
Feeling for another
Who cannot or will not feel
Hoping for another
Why endure the unnecessary pain
Because you never learn that there is no use
Caring for the careless
Feeling for those without feelings
Hoping for the hopeless
Pain is all there ever is
Pain is all there'll ever be

Abysmal

Why must it be so painful
Why so confusing
All rational thoughts
All rational actions
Lost
Leaving only misgivings and delusions
Broken promises and scams
More pain and suffering
Loss of trust and hope
Does it always have to be this way
I just wish it would end

Shades

There are many shades of day and night
Many shades of happiness and sorrow
To what extent
No one but the seer, sees
Or the feeler, feels
Only they know
Maybe they'll tell us tomorrow

Focus

As long as we keep in sight
What we feel to be wrong or right
Our feelings for one another will never alter
Albeit there will be times our tempers will flare
Our moods will falter
We may even lose sight of our goals
Never for long
Never too far from an arms grasp
As long as we keep in sight
Our love will always be strong and right

Moving On

I'm feeling so alone now
Left empty, hurt, and weary
I grew tired of fighting
I left behind the deception and lies
I'm leaving behind the pain and self-pity
Along with the feelings of rejection
As I go
I feel a heavy load lifting
An inner strength building
I feel at ease
Yet very much alone
In time
I will recover and bounce back
But always have a void within myself
For there will always be a place for you in my heart

My Oh My

The room is warm with your presence
A waft carries your scent filling my mind with you
My skin quivers with the slightest touch
My lips await your passionate kiss
My body yearns to be pressed against yours in the embrace of one
The thought of having you inside me overwhelms me
My mind reels
My pulse quickens
You inhabit my thoughts
Dwell in my dreams
Permeate my future
Without you nothing is truly complete
Nights are colder
Days are endless
Sleep is restless

What Happened

It started in a whirlwind
A whirlwind of passion
Fire and verve
I knew it wouldn't last
I knew it was just a fling
I knew it would be fun and done
I knew nothing
Now I know
I know about intensity
I know about true passion
I know about love
I know I get lost in your eyes
I know I melt from your touch
I know it's not just a fling
I know now I will never be done

Switched

I think we have switched
When I think about you a feeling comes over me
and I get chills
Goose bumps in anticipation
Sense of elation with memories
Shuddering now with regret
The thought of you being with another makes me shudder
I want to be the one you hold while you sleep
I want to be why you smile
I want you to become elated with thoughts of me
The feeling is overwhelming
I feel the tears welling in my eyes
My heart is skipping
My pulse is racing
My mind is reeling
My body is shuddering
All roads led me to you
You are my one

My Love

My love comes with baggage
My heart
My mind
My body
I feel deeply and strongly
I give of myself freely
I ask in return for your affection
I ask that you forgive
Forgive my insatiable desire
Forgive my persistence
Forgive my need for your touch
Your patience and understanding will be worth it
To you
I will give everything

Fuck You HAIKU

Fuck this
Fuck you
You inconsiderate bastard
I was stupid to believe anything you ever said
I was naive to trust you
Fuck you for just not caring
You hurt me, again
No more
No more time wasted on you
No more thoughts or ideas of what could be
Fuck me for falling
I'm done
Done caring
Done feeling
Done wanting
Done with you
Fuck this and
FUCK YOU

You Asked

You asked what I missed
I didn't answer
It would leave me open and vulnerable
The "feelings"
Too volatile
To Say
I missed your strong gentle touch
The feel of your lips against mine
The taste of you
The passion of your kiss
I missed the smell of you
The weight of your body lying on mine
The feel of your skin
The soothing sensual sound of your voice when you whisper my name
I missed the gaze we share when our eyes lock
I missed the turn of your mouth when only half a smile will do
I missed the longing look in your eyes
That face that always says there is something more I want to say.
I missed everything about you
Would be saying too much
I thought what we had was fleeting
That time away would be enough to satiate the fire within
I was so very wrong
When we are together
I can't imagine being anywhere else with anyone else
You are dangerous for me
I want what I can't have
But

I will always respect you and your wishes.
Now you know
What I didn't want to say

Say When

Say when you have had enough and it's time to stop
Say when you are no longer feeling as you did
Say when time is no longer too short
Say when you no longer care
Say when I no longer make you breathless
When it's over
Please just Say When

I Can Walk Away

My chest aches
My heart hurts
My eyes are finally dry
I've cried you out
Out of my heart
Out of my life
I can walk away now
Truly no vestige of hope remains
I no longer believe the sweet nothings
I no longer trust the convincing words
I've seen the future
Your not in it
I feel only the sorrow of what could have been
The loss of what will never be
You gambled the future
You lost
The spell is broken
I loved you
I love you
Now I'm moving on

Dangerous Desire

You evil bastard
You speak sweet nothings with your forked tongue
The look through your slitted eyes is hypnotizing
The breath you expel is acrid and addictive
Your touch burns and scintillates
The thought of you repulses and entices
I hate your look so Dark and sexy
You are repulsive and irresistible
An enigma of pain and undeniable pleasure
I curse your name and beg for your attention
Your hideous and delectable
I'm infected by you
My desire for you has no cure
The addiction is maddening
Cacoethes incarnate
Irrepressible pain
Undeniable attraction

Staying In Stasis

Staying in Stasis
Spiraling to nowhere
Everything is different
Nothing has changed
Time is elapsing
Scenery transforming
Life continues
Stuck in my own purgatory
Self induced stagnation
Refusing to go back
Afraid to move ahead
Frozen in a quagmire
Flight or fight has engaged
But Will has drained away
The grey is encroaching
Hopes light is dim
The glass is empty and broken
The door had been boarded up
Windows nailed shut
Staying in Stasis
For now is Safest

Everything Has Changed

Everything has changed
Yet it is all the same
Time goes on
But nothing changes
It is a circle
Never ending woe
It is not what I thought
Only what I know
I expected
I guess I even planned
No surprises here
Only a sad fear
That time won't stand still
And nothing will change

Decisions

Choices made under duress
Should I
Could I
Do I even want to
Am I happy
Or just settling
Can I be happy
Should I even try
What to do
How to act
What to think
Don't know
Unsure
Too many decisions
Choices to be made under duress

Alone

Alone I am
Alone I'll be
Not knowing who to love
Or who will love me
Choosing wrong
Without a thought
Choosing Right
Never
Naught
I don't know how to be anyway but alone
So, alone I am
Alone I will be

Agony

Pain is inevitable
Beit physical
Or, the much worse emotional
Time does not slow the infernal burn
Time does not make each day bearable
Time is but pain's henchman
Because time only makes the pain endure longer
There is no solution for pain
The cure is nonexistent
Pain is inevitable
Time its henchman
All that is left is emptiness
Endure or die

Made By My Choices

I feel so alone
The place I'm in is so vast and empty
No lights to brighten my way
No sound to lead me out
Only silence and darkness
An abyss of loneliness
I'm drowning in the desert
Thirsting in an oasis
Suffering in paradise
Loneliness is my anchor
Holding me to this forsaken place
I call my nesting ground
How do I shake this Albatross
This self induced prison
Made by my choices
My indiscretions
My mistakes
When will I learn
My world is asunder

Wasted Effort

It's all lost on you
My time
My heart
My thoughts
My love
It has been a waste
The planning
The excitement
You appreciate nothing
And give nothing in return
I ask for understanding
I get exasperation
I ask for time
I get excuses
I beg for compassion
I get extreme indifference
My heart is lost on you
My love a waste
I want to give
You only take
You took my heart
You took my love
You took my spirit
There is nothing left to take

My Anger, My Friend

My anger wells inside of me
Yearning for release
Opting for destruction of all in its path
Unbridled
Untamed
Unrelenting
I can't control or confine it
It engulfs and consoles me
Comforts in times of disappointment
Coddles during loneliness
Protects in times of danger
My anger is my friend
I long for its fiery embrace
It fights the tears
It decimates the weakness
My one true reliable friend
Dependable
Persistent
Consistent
My Anger
My friend

Vows to Remember

With you this day I share my love
I give to you all that I am or will ever be
I have nothing that is not yours
I live to share with you all that I can
I need you to grow with me
I trust that you will always be there for me
I know with each day our love will grow and flourish
I dedicate my heart and soul to you
All that I am
All that I will ever be
Is yours
Open your heart and arms
Embrace Me
Cherish Me
Love Me
For all eternity

Rut or Bust

My heart is in turmoil
My life is in a rut
I know that I am missing something
As of yet I don't know what
Maybe I will find it
Maybe I never will
Until the time when something comes about
Be it death or a new understanding
My heart will stay in turmoil
My life will stay in a rut

Loneliness

Loneliness
Even the word is sad
It's a feeling of being alone
A fear that you'll stay that way
A void that needs to be filled
An emotion that spares no one
To feel this is to truly be alone
It's hard to shake
Even harder to fix
Maybe One day
Hopefully Some day
The pain from the void will go away

Bah Humbug

Christmas, Bah Humbug
Overrated
Over priced
Just plain senseless
It's a time for let downs
A time for sorrow
Supposedly
A time for happiness and cheer
But if you're all alone
It's the worst time of the year

Life

Time comes
Time goes
Leaving you full of woe
Wondering
How
Why
Should I live
Should I die
Will it worsen
Will it get better
I ask the questions
No answers
Only silence
My only solace
I won't live forever

Seeking

Why is it so hard
To find one to love
Who will love you in return
Someone who wants you as you want them
Why must it always be so wrong
So hard
So impossible
I have tried and don't care to try anymore
I give up
I quit
No longer will I put myself through this pain
If only I could
But I need someone
I need to be needed

Roadmap to Eternity

Time spent away from you
Is time spent longing
My mind reels with thoughts of you
I can feel your touch in your absence
Your scent makes me quiver in anticipation and yearning
My dreams and thoughts are of you
I wake and my first thought is of you
I lay down at night thinking of you
You are first and foremost in my heart
The thought of losing you disheartens me
Your absence troubles me
I think of no one but you
I can't envision a future without you
You make the days bearable
The nights desirable
My beacon in the darkness
I need you in my life

Broke Down

I feel lost again
Adrift in a sea of confusion
Every turn leads back to the beginning
Every road a dead end
No lights
No signs
No directions
No out in sight
So
I stop
I park
I wait
No one stops to see
No one comes to help
Broke down on life's highway
Stranded on my mind's deserted road

Emotional X-Ray

These eyes of mine have shed many tears
This heart of mine has felt many fears
I've tried to be strong
I've tried to look away
I've tried to hide what I couldn't say
In the end
I lost what I tried so hard to keep
Left feeling lonely and weak
I felt drained
I felt alone
I knew in fact I was on my own
So, if you are wondering what makes me, me
Look past the obvious
See past the facade
Understand what's deep inside of me

I Don't Understand

I feel much confusion and pain
Its source I cannot name
I hear the words you say to me
My mind won't let me perceive them
I feel the things you do to me
My heart wants to believe them
My body turns against itself
My heart one way
My mind another
When will all this madness end
Why can't we just be together

Internal Turmoil

It's so hard to love
To have your heart hurt
Your brain fighting within itself
Your stomach twisted in permanent knots
Is it worth it
All the pain and anguish
Sometimes No
Sometimes Yes
To feel an empty void in your heart filled
To feel your mind at peace
To have your stomach filled with butterflies instead of knots
To feel that certain glow and warmth
To have the need to be needed and wanted fulfilled
Supposedly the ultimate of all feelings
Is it
Sometimes Yes
Sometimes No
Me personally, I don't think so

Barely Getting By

It's over
Done
Finished
What do I do now
I do nothing
There is nothing left to do
Where do I go now
I go nowhere
Because I have been there so many times before
How do I feel now
I feel lost
I feel totally alone
I feel relief
When I allow time to feel
What should have lasted eternally
Ended in grief
What should have been unfettered bliss
Was laced with arsenic and anger
It's finally over
It's finished
I'm done
I will do as I've always done
Go On

Forbidden Fruit

I have a feeling inside of me
It's growing with each passing day
The more I see you
The more I want you
To feel your hands caressing me
To Feel your body intertwined with mine
To feel your lips brushing mine in the beginnings of
a passionate kiss
These are the thoughts that surface over and over
again
Every time I catch a glimpse of you
I can't get rid of the old and bring in the new
You see, I want a married man
Forbidden fruit
And that's very old for me

BOOM

The sound was deafening
The pain incomprehensible
The ache deep and throbbing
My mind was rationalizing
But my heart was broken
The words physically took shape and punched me
The barrage of words and blows
Incapacitated me
I was hurt
Lost
Dumbfounded
You Cheated

Real Man's Praise

A man I know
He's there for support
He's there for fun
He's there for me in times of need
The man I know
Cares deeply
Feels strongly
Loves unconditionally
The man I know
Is strong in heart
Quick in mind
Sure In spirit
That man I know
Is true
Is reliable
Is my eternal friend
The man I trust
A friend for life

Sometimes

Sometimes I think of what was
Sometimes I think of what will be
Most of the times I just have problems coping with
Realty
You might say I'm mixed up
You may say I'm odd
But none of that matters to me
I am who I am
I'll be who I'll be

GRRRRRRRR

I can't change
I won't change
I will not break or bend
It's not me
It will never be
I can't be what you want me to be
I can only be me
Deal with it if you can
Leave, if you can't
Because
I will not be broken
I will not be bent

Destitute

Lost and alone
I am
Confused and distraught
I stay
Lonely and forlorn
I've become
Can I change it
I cannot
Tried and failed
I am done
Alone and lost
I will remain

Let It Go

I love you too much
To ever start liking you
Let's just let the story end
Please
Don't expect me to be your friend

Guidance Required

My mind is in turmoil
My heart in a bind
I feel detached and guilt ridden
I say I'm in love
But I don't act it
I know I want to be
But I can't show it
When left on my own
I act shameless
When together
I'm devoted and true
I hate being away
But I miss the freedom
I don't know what I want
But being alone is not an option
I'm fickle and out of control
I need a firm guiding hand
To lend control and structure
Bring together what is separate
Make right my wrongs
Set straight my deviated path
But I balk under authority
I want to be something I'm not sure I'm capable of being
I will continue to try
But to what avail

Lies, Deception, Betrayal

Lies
Deception
Betrayal
To what end
For what purpose
Lies only delay the imminent
Deception just masks the inevitable
Betrayal, alas Salts the wound
Nothing is gained
Nothing is avoided
Pain becomes exponential
Truth is the only outlet
Truth allows wounds to heal
Truth allows passage to Euphoria
Lies
Deception
Betrayal
A decimating trio

Poisonous Comfort

I detest my heart
It betrays at every avenue
It makes the caustic desirable
I hate my feelings
They allow such pain to overwhelm and incapacitate
I abhor the love I have for you
For it makes me weak and indecisive
I hate my arms
Because they ache to hold you
I detest my eyes
Because they are blinded by you
I abhor my feet
Because they run after you
I am disgusted with myself
Because I have forsaken myself for you

Pondering Me

I know who I am
I think
I know where I've been
I query
I know what I've done
I regret
I've been, done and seen
But still I ponder
Who I am
Where I'm going
What will I do
I'm not sure
I'm not ready
How can I prepare
What lies ahead
Will I be able to deal
Will there be more regrets
Will these myriad of questions abate
Flip Side
Love is a splendid thing
When it is felt by both involved
Yet
Love can be a knife twisting in your very soul
When it is felt by only one
Let it go and try again

Growing Pains

The time we have shared
Wrought with pain and passion
Love and hate
Anger and forgiveness
Time wasted
No
Time well spent
Living
Learning
Loving
Fighting
Failing
Forgiving
Growing beyond even our own boundaries
Making mistakes and finding solutions

Anticipation of Beginning

I want you so much
I can't sleep
I can't think straight
My mind wanders with thoughts of you
My arms ache to hold and embrace you
My lips quiver awaiting your touch
My body, well my body just yearns
I want these feelings to ebb, pass, or go away
Just so I can make it through the day
I miss the warmth I can't share
I miss the arms that used to hold me
Hell, I just miss you
I want to spend my nights in your arms
And days in your gaze
I need to escape this abyss of emptiness and loneliness
As long as I breathe I ache
Until I am back in your embrace
I want the different world to go away
So, We can begin our life

Chasing IT

The rush is maddening
The overwhelming waves of emotion
There are times I can't breathe
Days I can't think
I feel like I'm drowning in it
Suffocating under the weight of it
Some days I hate it
Others I long for it
Today I'm perplexed by it
Always in the distance
Just out of reach
At times so close I can almost touch it
Others so far away it seems only a speck on the horizon
I've eluded to it in my dreams
I believe I've even brushed against it
Never truly possessing it
Always slipping out my grasp
Hell
Half the time I don't even know what it is
All I know
I want It
One day
I will have IT
Hopefully, I will know what to do with IT

Perpetually Packed

A Life constantly in transition
Never unpacking
No setting roots
No home
No one to call my own
Bothersome
Sometimes
Lonely
Mostly
Freedom has a price
No commitments
No ties
Free to be
ALONE
Loving it only because it is
Accept what is
Embrace transition
Freedom
To be
To do
Nomadic in nature
Tortured in spirit
Wanting in body
Perpetually packed
Explains a life constantly in transition

Broken

I'm broken
Eyes filling
Body aching
Mind reeling
Heart shattered
Pain nonstop
Mental
Physical
Spiritual
No out
Nothing else matters
No one else knows
The pain
No one sees
No one cares
The earth spins
The clock ticks
The sun rises
Anguish continues
Screams unheard
Tears unshed
Words unspoken

Ode to Reko

It hurts
To think of you
To feel the pain no weapon can inflict
A dull throbbing ache
Growing in intensity with every breath
Every thought cuts deep
Memories are scars ripped open and kept oozing
Lamenting over lost time together
Regretting missed opportunities not taken
The pain of loss never heals
However
The tears do stop
The hurt does abate
The heart wound does close and scar
And the rest of life without you
Continues On

Simple

It doesn't have to be complicated
Does it
Time spent enjoying the company of another
Is enough
Kisses shared between two inviting lips
Touches passed from one to another when the feeling arises
Satisfying
Two people
Two lives
All aspects need not be intertwined
Love can blossom in the harshest of environments
or the most fertile of lands
It doesn't follow a script
So why write one
Accept it as it comes
Open your eyes
Open your heart
If doesn't have to be complicated
Unless
You want it to be

Spiraling

I just need out of this moment
I know
It won't last
I know
It will get better
I know
I know
But I can't
It's so dark
There is nothing
No light
No hope
No need to go on
If only this moment will pass
I'm trying to wait
I'm hoping
Fuck, I'm praying
The darkness is closing in
The hopelessness consuming
This moment continuing unreleasing
Damn this moment
Fuck this feeling
Fuck this life
This time
This moment
I need peace
I desperately need this moment to pass
SO
I can breathe
I can feel the light
I can sense the hope
I cannot quit
I can go on
It Passed
For Now

The Taste Of Impending Pain

Your taste is divine
The sweet smell of you
Skin soft and supple beneath my fingers
I trace the curves of your body with my tongue
My mouth waters thinking of you
Longing to touch you
Starving to taste
My body yearns for you
My heart breaks for you
The pain I sense
Bittersweet tears I taste
Only you know
Only you can share
I'm here for you
In spirit
In space
I'll wait

Hierarchy of Needs

Love with an unbound heart

Accept and understand that you are at the core of
my thoughts and deeds

Know my body is yours to explore and indulge from
toe to tip

Embrace the uniqueness that is me and practice
the patience that encompasses the same

Feel my needs and act without the hesitancy
because we are one

My ask is simple and complete
For it you will have totality
You will have me

Delusion

You're an Idiot
Too Misguided
Too Blind to see
So Smart you're Stupid
A Walking, talking PSA
Bricks falling all around you
Sirens wailing into deaf ears
Lights flashing into unseeing eyes
The truth is lost on you
Living in your Dream world
Built with bricks of Denial
Secured with mortar of Make Believe
This oxymoronic predicament
Time wasted and well spent
I give up before I explode into nothingness
I've succumbed to the stupidity of it all
I don't want to catch the inane
I was long ago vaccinated against absurdity
I've accepted and peace has ensued
What a fucking joke you are

Ode to You

Roses are Red
Violets are Blue
I'm a sock
My sister my shoe

Strong embrace covers to keep me safe
Ties to keep me grounded
Treads to give me traction to propel me forward
Support to bear the weight of me

Daisies are Yellow
Grass is Green
My socks are mismatched
But my Roots are Pristine

Origin of One

We are all Africans
Borne of one continent
Divided over time
We all come from the same Mother Earth
We all succumb to Father Time
Our Blood flows red
Our hearts beat to the same metronomic rhythm
How does hating yourself come easy
Does pallor promote prejudice
Does eye color blind the beholder to rational thought
Is the depth of one's character determined by the pigment of an inch of skin
It's ridiculous
Simply Insane to think any of it matters
Race
Religion
Orientation
Gender
We are supposedly Sentient
But we waste on hate
Our Mother bore us
Our Father ages us
Our experience wisens us
Our hate weakens us
Our actions define Us
History will remember Us
All that remains is gray dust

The Middle

What happens in the middle
Words flow like water in the beginning
The Newness
The Learning
The hope of loving
Words fly like Daggers in the End
The Anger
The Stagnation
The ache of longing
Words come so difficult in the Middle
They can't form into the thoughts that explain it all
The silence speaking what words cannot
The fear of offending
The frustration of not being heard
The regret of feelings unsaid
Silence causing it to slowly slip away
The beginning dialogue flowing and growing
The ending shouts cutting and destroying
If only a few simple words could be spoken
Salvation could be had
If only the taking for granted didn't breed complacency
Light could shine through
If only you could Say
Mouths open with stilled tongues
What matters most never heard
The Deepest cuts left festering and oozing
Apathy sets in and the venom flows
Novelty is freedom
Familiarity Contempt
In the Middle lies that chasm
Words the Bridge

Think It Through

What's wrong with Now
Time is Relative
Feelings are real
We clicked and knew it
Loyalty is double edged
It cuts deep but not clean
Earning it is constant
Not a One and Done
Resting on laurels is bullshit
Everyday deposits must be made in the Loyalty Trust
Fools reward the past without acknowledging the present
Sagacity remembers what was and prizes what is
Wake Up
Realize
Loss is imminent
Choose Wisely

Bursted Bubbles

So many regrets
Opportunities lost
Time spent
Hands empty
Mind filled
The thoughts abound
What could have been
What should have been
Time wasn't in sync
I am not to blame
I gave
You took
I chose to see what could be
Looked past what was in front of me
I saw the good and possible
You were the film that clouded my perceptive lens
I knew and pushed aside
I felt and shrugged away
Fuck forgiveness
You siphoned my love and left a husk
What should have energized and revitalized
Has drained and pilfered
My heart of joy
My soul of glow
My eyes of light
The opaque film is gone
I see you for the beast you are
Be gone
Be well
Be forgotten

The Package

You know it doesn't exist
Right
You know
The Package
The Perfect person
The One
Listens with no judgement
Feels with no abandon
Loves unconditionally
Speaks and Does
There when you need them
Support in the storm
They're just a figment
Dreamt from a feeble mind
Desperate for what can never be
Deluded into thinking
Duped into believing they ever existed
Cellulose creations
Lyrical lies
Walking talking words on pages
Made up mates
Ports in mental storms
Hope for the emotionally drowning
An extended hand to lift the beaten down
Realize
They don't exist
Expect nothing get nothing
Skirt disappointment
Elude the anguish
Be who you need them to be